PIÑATA SMASH LINGS™

The Official
SMASHLINGS
COLLECTOR'S
GUIDE

Andrews McMeel
PUBLISHING®

Andrews McMeel Publishing
a division of Andrews McMeel Universal
1130 Walnut Street, Kansas City, Missouri 64106

www.andrewsmcmeel.com

24 25 26 27 28 SDB 10 9 8 7 6 5 4 3 2 1
ISBN: 978-1-5248-9371-2
Library of Congress Control Number: 2023951128

Editor: Erinn Pascal
Assistant Editor: Cindy Harris
Production Editor: Jennifer Straub
Production Manager: Julie Skalla

Made by:
RR Donnelley (Guangdong) Printing Solutions Company Ltd.
Address and location of manufacturer:
No. 2 Minzhu Road, Daning, Humen Town,
Dongguan City, Guangdong Province, China 523930
1st Printing—1/22/2024

ATTENTION: SCHOOLS AND BUSINESSES
Andrews McMeel books are available at quantity discounts with bulk purchase for
educational, business, or sales promotional use. For information, please e-mail the
Andrews McMeel Publishing Special Sales Department: sales@amuniversal.com.

CONTENTS

WELCOME TO THE

Piñata Smashlings is a super fun party world, ready and waiting for you to explore!

Jump aboard the magnificent flying Rainbow Whale as it soars above the Piñataverse, showering every corner of the land with Rainbow Pods. It's here where the adventure really begins as you chase, catch, and hatch the colorful pods. Inside each pod awaits an excitable Smashling! There are lots of these adorable little characters to collect, and you can discover tons of fun facts about them on pages 42 to 160 of this book.

PIÑATAVERSE

Use the map and location guides on pages 26 to 41 to help you explore the expansive and ever-growing world, and you'll soon discover that not everything is sweetness and light. Darkness looms with menacing Meañatas up to no good, turning Smashlings into bitter Bashlings, but luckily there are Piñatas to help save the day! Make sure you read all about these characters on pages 10 to 23, so you know what you're up against.

So, what are you waiting for? Turn the page and get ready to discover and learn more about the wonderful world of Piñata Smashlings . . . .

RAINBOW WHALE

Flying happily over the skies of the Piñataverse is the incredible Rainbow Whale. Some believe this magnificent creature nests in The Great Tree, but no one knows for sure. It's the greatest mystery there is.

When the Rainbow Whale is in town, there is much excitement. It means one thing . . . the Rainbow Whale is about to magically deliver the Rainbow Pods!

RAINBOW PODS

Inside each of these colorful pods is a Smashling! The Rainbow Whale delivers Rainbow Pods randomly all over the Piñataverse. It causes a huge frenzy to catch, hatch, and befriend the Smashlings inside.

DID YOU KNOW?
It's a common sight to see a Smashling's legs poking through its Rainbow Pod and running around in all directions.

SMASHLINGS

These energetic little creatures can be spotted gallivanting all over the Piñataverse and having lots of adventures. Each Smashling is different and has its own unique personality. The adorable beings all have individual character traits, likes, dislikes, and besties they hang out and party with.

Most Smashlings you'll meet are positive, sweet, friendly, good, fun-loving, and always ready to **PARTY!**

BASHLINGS

Bashlings are Smashlings turned bitter. They are mischievous party-poopers looking to ruin the Smashlings' fun. Bashlings help the Meañatas catch and chase down Rainbow Pods and Smashlings to turn them into Bashlings.

About: Bitter, grumpy, selfish, manipulative, and argumentative

DID YOU KNOW? Soaking a Bashling with water from the Rainbow River can turn it back into a Smashling. Water balloons and blasters work well for this.

Gruel began to change!

And Gruel, the first Bashling, was born!

PIÑATAS

These larger-than-life creatures look out for the Smashlings, offering guidance and shielding them from the Meañatas and Bashlings. The Piñatas, with their positive and vibrant nature, bring a blend of trust and order to the Piñataverse. They never go on missions, but they always give good advice. One day, the Smashlings might even listen to it.

TIP
Keep an eye out for your favorite Piñata as you explore the Piñata Village.

WATCH OUT!

Piñatas avoid venturing into the Swamplands because it is dark and scary. It is particularly dangerous on nights when there is a full Piñata moon.

Dazzle is super-protective of Smashlings and has a powerful kick when threatened. Many Meañatas have been on the receiving end of this Dizzy Donkey.
HEE-HAW!

About:
Trustworthy, respectful, and dizzy

DID YOU KNOW?
Dazzle is the mayor of Piñata Village and greets all visitors with a warm welcome.

DAZZLE
THE DIZZY DONKEY PIÑATA

Dizzy by name, dizzy by nature, Dazzle the Dizzy Donkey loves nothing more than spinning uncontrollably until it falls in a crumpled heap on the floor. No one really knows why it does this, but it's widely believed that Dazzle just loves joy, laughter, and the feeling of giddiness as its tassels move freely with the motion. Even though Dazzle can act somewhat silly, this mule is no fool—it can become extremely focused and razor-sharp alert seemingly out of nowhere. Surprise!

FUN FACT

Luna is one of the few Piñatas that isn't afraid of the dark, gloomy atmosphere of the Swamplands.

LUNA
THE STARLIGHT UNICORN PIÑATA

Luna is a positive Piñata and a great friend to all. Super-rare Starlight Unicorn Piñatas are very handy to have around, especially in the dark, as they have the unique ability to control light! Luna can use the star at the end of its piñata stick as a bright and powerful light source, and no other Piñata can do this. Like all Piñatas, Luna keeps a close eye over the Smashlings to keep them safe.

About: Honest, strong, and thoughtful

FUN FACT

Drinking marzimoo milk has a very calming effect. The milk is collected by squeezing the buds of the marzimoo plant. A saucer of marzimoo milk could easily distract Mo, but luckily the baddies haven't worked this out yet!

MO
THE QUICK STICK TIGER PIÑATA

Mo believes in teamwork and operates in unison with the other Piñatas to protect the Smashlings against the bitterness that lurks.

It dislikes heights and is one of the only Piñatas to fear a ride on the Rainbow Whale. When it comes to flying, only a large helping of marzimoo milk can calm this big kitty down. Mo is no scaredy cat though, for this proud Piñata relishes showing off its strength and never backs down from a challenge.

SANA
THE PEACEFUL PANDA PIÑATA

Sana is a wise Piñata able to keep balance and sweetness across the Piñataverse. Often voyaging high up into the caves of the Marshmallow Mountains to find enlightenment, this Peaceful Panda Piñata has a strong connection with the Rainbow Energy that flows throughout the lands. It is stronger than any other Piñata. This is why Sana's number-one duty is warding off the terrible Meañatas and their attempts to disrupt peace and spread bitterness.

FUN FACT

Sana is a bamboo master, but spends more time chewing on its bamboo stick than using it to swipe things with.

About: Balanced, mindful, and harmonious

MEAÑATAS

With an evil agenda of ridding the Piñataverse of fun for everyone, Meañatas are Piñatas turned bad. Meañatas scheme to catch and cage Smashlings. They send out their Bashling minions to spy on and trick Smashlings into visiting the Swamplands, where they are caught and turned into Bashlings.

NOT SO FUN FACT
Smashlings can only be turned into Bashlings when there is a full Piñata moon in the Swamplands. Captured Smashlings are kept in cages until then.

DID YOU KNOW?
Meañatas and Bashlings wear hoods to stop water from the Rainbow River from washing away their bitterness.

THE ECOSYSTEM

The Piñataverse is home to Piñatas, Meañatas, Smashlings, and Bashlings. Smashlings hatch from Rainbow Pods dropped by the magical Rainbow Whale.

The Rainbow Whale drops Rainbow Pods.

Smashlings and Bashlings race for the Pods.

Smashlings are sweet, fun-loving, and full of party spirit.

Bitter Bashlings want to help the evil Meañatas turn Smashlings into Bashlings.

Piñatas keep a watchful eye over the Smashlings, like an older sibling, and protect them against Meañatas.

Meañatas try to snatch Smashlings and turn them into bitter Bashlings.

CHARMS, FRUITIES, AND GEMS

CHARMS

Charms are collectible items. Smashlings love charms because they make the world more

TIP

Make sure you have enough Fruities to tame a Smashling!

FRUITIES

Seen all over the Piñataverse, Fruities come in various mouth-watering shapes and colors. They can be found inside sweet surprise piñatas that spawn across the map and can be broken up as an explosion of rewards! Fruities are used to feed and tame Smashlings so you can add them to collections.

GEMS

Not as plentiful as Fruities, Gems can be found in just a few places around the Piñataverse. They are given as rewards for quests and can be used to upgrade tools and get Smashlings.

MAP OF THE PIÑATAVERSE

Marvel at the map of the Piñataverse, and then read about some of its special magical places on pages 28 to 37.

Root Village

Rainbow Road

Smashling Seas

Piñata Village

Desert Dunes

Mecha Zone

Wavy Ways

Sherbert Shores

The Great Tree

Marshmallow Mountains

Mable the Talking Tree

Mt. Meañata

Rainbow Plateau

Rumble Jungle

The Swamplands

Candy Cliffs

PIÑATA VILLAGE

Enter the main bustling hub of the Piñataverse—the Piñata Village! This is where you might bump into some of the Piñatas and Mable the Talking Tree to receive your quests. You can also shop for tools, furniture, and other items, and upgrade Smashlings in the training dojo. It's also where you'll find all the latest info on all the Piñataverse events!

MABLE THE TALKING TREE

Mable is a glorious golden maple-syrup tree. Ancient and wise, Mable is the place to go for information and quests. It's also a great place to meet friends. At the foot of Mable is an enchanting Rainbow Wishing Well that's used to complete some of the quests.

THE GREAT TREE

Travel north over Marshmallow Mountains and you'll stand on the east side of the most impressive and mysterious tree you'll ever come across. This tree is mahoosive and can be seen from anywhere on the main island. Smashlings use The Great Tree as a compass to navigate around the Piñataverse. According to local legend, the Rainbow Whale makes its nest at the tippity top of this towering tree, but no one knows for sure.

FUN FACT

The Great Tree is a popular destination for climbers, tourists, and adventurers such as Pip and Captain Buck.

ROOT VILLAGE

Hidden in dense undergrowth somewhere near the base of The Great Tree is Root Village. Here, Smashlings are hidden from prying Meañatas and Bashlings. The village is the Smashlings' best-kept secret. **SHH!**

TREE HOUSES

From the outside, you might be mistaken into thinking that all tree houses are the same, but don't be fooled! Most Smashlings individually tailor their homes to reflect their personalities. Some are lavish with many different rooms and levels, while others prefer the simplicity of a minimal tree house. It's all down to personal taste.

MECHA ZONE

The high-tech Mecha Zone is mainly inhabited by Bot Smashlings. It's THE place to find the latest gadgets and innovations—everything from high-speed bumper cars to energy cells charged by Rainbow Water.

DID YOU KNOW?

If you're passing through the Mecha Zone, keep an eye out for Garby, a Dumpster Trunk Smashling that keeps the area free of litter and is responsible for the recycling.

TIP

You can visit the Mecha Zone Water Park and take a slide on the Water Wowler—the largest water slide in the Piñataverse!

If you're in the market for a new bumper car, check out Boarsy's second-hand car dealership.

(*Disclaimer: This is a paid advertisement from Boarsy.)

MONSTER DEALS! THAT CAN'T BE BEATEN

TIP

If you find yourself deep in the heart of the jungle, you may stumble upon an ancient artifact or disused cave dwelling from a long-lost civilization. Exciting, yes, but it's probably best to take an experienced adventurer like Captain Buck to guide you through.

RUMBLE JUNGLE

Epic adventure awaits here! With much of the Piñataverse jungle left unexplored, the Rumble Jungle is an adventurer's dream. It's also the best place to play hide-and-seek, so long as you don't stray too deep and get tangled up in juicy jungle fruit vines. Yikes!

THE RAINBOW RIVER

FUN FACT

Meañatas and Bashlings that bathe in the Rainbow River will turn sweet again.

Flowing fabulously throughout most of the Piñataverse, the Rainbow River is an amazing network of magical water.

DID YOU KNOW?
The Swamplands is the only place where the Rainbow River doesn't flow.

OMG

35

THE SWAMPLANDS

LOOMS AND GLOOMS

Looms are mischievous red toadstools that wander all over the forests. Many happy-go-lucky Looms have strolled off into the Swamplands and changed to grumpy green stinkers. These Looms are then known as Glooms—Looms turned bitter. Not only do they smell foul, but their pranks are a lot more sinister.

This dark and dingy place is full of terror and all things b-b-b-bad. Deep in the Swampland's murky depths lies the Meañatas' hideout. Only the bravest (or silliest) of Smashlings would ever dare to enter the Swamplands. At the very heart of this horrifying place is an oozing, stinky central swamp that all bitterness and evil spreads out from.

NOT SO FUN FACT

If the swamp grows enough, it could overpower the Rainbow River and cause it to dull, thicken, and become swamp-like as well.

PIÑATA PARTY BUS

FUN FACT

The on-board dance floor in the Party Bus has enough room for even the most enthusiastic dancer to show off their groovy moves!

DID YOU KNOW?

Pooks is a spray-paint master and created the artwork that gives the Party Bus its disco vibes.

Nothing gets the party started like the ultimate blast on wheels—the Piñata Party Bus! Smashlings come from far and wide to cut loose and groove under the disco ball, as this incredible party destination pumps out sweet tunes that can be heard from miles around!

YUM TRUCK

Rrrrrrumble! Grrruummmble! Is that the sound of Mt. Meañata about to erupt? No, it's actually the hungry growl of a Smashling's stomach between meals. But fear not, famished friends, the Yum Truck is never too far away and is always ready to supply mouth-watering treats to ravenous Smashlings.

FUN FACT

An ice-cold giggle juice is perfect for washing down any of the yummiest of treats at the Yum Truck. Just don't be surprised if you have to wait in line, as every Smashling loves visiting this marvelous machine!

DID YOU KNOW?

Hammy and its friends have a superb selection of the Piñataverse's finest fare, from triple-decker fire fruit burgers to sweet marzimoo milk treats.

MY SMASHLINGS COLLECTION

How big is your Smashling collection? Check them off as you collect each one!

BEEP BOOP	BERRY BOO	BLOB

BLOOPY	BLUSH	BOARSY	BUMPS	BUNKINS	CAPTAIN BUCK	CHA CHA
CHEEP CHEEP	CHERRY BLOOM	CHERRY BUN	CHEWY	CHUCK	COLIN	CONKS
CRUMBLES	CUDDLES	DASH	DEARIE	DORIS	DRAKE 	DROPLET
DUSTY	ELLA	EL GRANDE POCO	FANKLE	FERN	FIZZ POP	FLAKES
FLUFFS	FRANKLIN	GARBY	GIGGLES	GRIBBY	GRUFF	GUS
HAMMY	HAZ	HELPY	HERBY	HONEY	JASPER	JET

KEE WEE	KIKI	KNUCKLES	LAZE	LEAKY	LOL	LOLLY

LOU LOU	MARSH	MELLOW	MELTSY	MELV	MEOW	MINI BLUE

MOONLET	NELSON	NOAKS	OMG	PARPY	PATSY	PIP

POCA JO JO	POOKS	PRICKLES	PUGGSY	RASKINS	RAY	RAYN

REGGIE	RICHIE	ROLLY	ROYDON	RUFF	RUS	SHAKEY

SHIVERS	SIX	SLURPY	SNOOTS	SOCKS	SPLATS	SPRINKLES

SQUEAK	SQUISH	STEGGY	STIG	STING	SWIRLY WURL	TUTAN

TUTTI BEL	TWINKY	TWIST	WAFFLES	WELLS	WIGGLES	WIMBLY

A Sound Bot Smashling

BEEP BOOP

Let's make some noise for the ultimate beat-boxing champ . . . Beep Boop! This super-loud Sound Bot Smashling and its bestie Drake, the HipHopper Potter Mouse, spend most of their time recording music and making albums together. Beep often surprises other Smashlings with a random **Pop! BANG! Whizzzz! Bark! or HONNKKK!** Luckily, most of them think it's funny and are amazed by its epic range of sounds.

About: Friendly, talkative, and playful
Rarity: Uncommon
Likes: Making noises
Dislikes: The sound of silence
Beep Boop's besties: Drake, Cheep Cheep, and Lou Lou

CHEEP CHEEP

LOU LOU

DRAKE

WHOOPS!

ARGGGG! GRRRRR! Sounds like poor Beep Boop has been tricked and turned into a Bashling! Hopefully it'll shuffle and slide its way to the Rainbow River and get back to making some sweet tunes!

45

DID YOU KNOW? When Friendly Fruit Smashlings grow white furry beards, they really itch!

A Friendly Fruit Smashling

BERRY BOO

Usually perfectly sweet and juicy, if left out in the sunshine for too long this Friendly Fruit grows a berry furry white beard. That's why you'll mainly find lovely Berry Boo staying cool at its excellent sandwich shop. This culinary whizz also loves experimenting with baking bread, cakes, pastries, and delicious snacks.

All of Berry Boo's sensational creations are in its famous recipe book, which is kept locked away in a secret hiding place. This is because of rumors that sneaky Bashlings are trying to steal it to create moldy versions of the recipes and turn Smashlings bitter. Yuck!

FUN FACT

Berry Boo makes the very best Wobbly Bobbly sandwich in the entire Piñataverse. Yum!

About: Friendly, busy, and helpful
Rarity: Uncommon
Likes: Baking
Dislikes: Growing a beard
Berry Boo's besties: Cherry Bloom, Colin, and Kee Wee

CHERRY BLOOM

Berry Boo's

COLIN

KEE WEE

FUN FACT

Golden Gobstopper Pearls can only be found deep at the bottom of the Smashific Ocean. Blob is on a mission to bring one home to Root Village, but so far has found little more than a smelly old boot.

BLOB

Blob is a Bobbing Wobbler Smashling—graceful in the water, but not so much on land. Bobbler Wobbler Smashlings wibble-wobble like a bowl of jello (which they find hilarious), flopping along from place to place. They also tend to be a bit wrinkly, like how your fingers get when you've been in the bath too long. It's no surprise really, as Bobbing Wobblers spend most of their time underwater. Blob loves deep-sea diving and travels far and wide across the Smashling Seas in search of Golden Gobstopper Pearls—the rarest and most valuable natural treasures known within the Piñataverse.

Blob's besties:

GUS   BLOOPY   SHIVERS

About: Adventurous, seafaring, and wobbly
Rarity: Epic
Likes: Deep-sea diving
Dislikes: Pirates

BLOOPY

Wahoo! This mega splashtastic Whalewoo Smashling is a water-slide enthusiast and, wowsers, what a splash Bloopy makes on the big slides at the Mecha Zone Water Park! Bloopy is a season ticket holder and massive fan of the wonderful Water Wowler, the largest slide.

About: Sniffly, bold, and perceptive
Rarity: Rare
Likes: Water parks
Dislikes: Beaches

DID YOU KNOW?

Whalewoos have a remarkable sense of direction, and Bloopy can easily locate the water park's food truck when it's on the move.

A Whalewoo Smashling

Bloopy's besties:

BLOB	GUS	SWIRLY WURL	CHERRY BUN

BLUSH

This sizzling-hot Smashling spends its time furiously flapping its tiny wings, soaring above the clouds across the Piñataverse skies looking for parties to join. Blazing Blush loves a party more than any Smashling, but be prepared for a fiery affair at Blush's own birthday bash. Have you ever seen a dragon blow out candles on a birthday cake? Let's just say, stand back and have a fire extinguisher at the ready.

A Sizzler Smashling

FUN FACT

Blush loves to roast marshmallows. "The more roasted, the better," Blush likes to say!

About: Energetic, assertive, and HOT TO THE TOUCH!
Rarity: Uncommon
Likes: Roasting marshmallows
Dislikes: Fire alarms
Blush's besties: Squeak, Sting, and Tutan

TUTAN

TOOT TOOT

STING

SQUEAK

WHOOPS!
Youch! It seems Blush has become a burning ball of all things bitter and bad. May it burn out soon!

BOARSY

Introducing Boarsy, a smooth-talking Selly Welly Smashling who's a car enthusiast and always ready to make you a deal. Looking for a great new vehicle? Step inside Boarsy's Mecha Zone Car Dealership. Boarsy boasts that its "monster deals can't be beaten anywhere in the Piñataverse." Boarsy can charm the pants off anyone, even Prince Charming from Charmsville, Planet Charm!

DID YOU KNOW?

Boarsy once sold The Great Tree to a Bashling! Of course, The Great Tree isn't for sale and can't be sold. Let's just say the gullible Bashling felt a bit silly when it found out.

A Selly Welly Smashling

FUN FACT

Boarsy has the only car dealership in the entire Piñataverse.

About: Charming, slick, and assertive
Rarity: Uncommon
Likes: Fast cars
Dislikes: A bad deal

Boarsy's besties:

HELPY	POOKS	TWIST

BUMPS

Watch out! This Tidy Slidey Smashling slides everywhere on its tummy. It's quite a sight! But Bumps seems to get it wrong most of the time, slipping and sliding around, over-shooting on the ice and thumping head-first into walls, or sliding off edges and into the sea.

FUN FACT

Bumps is safest in a pair of tap shoes. This Tidy Slidey sure can shuffle-hop-step-ball-change, and loves its tap dancing lessons every Tuesday afternoon.

About: Opinionated, accident-prone, and outgoing
Rarity: Rare
Likes: Tap dancing
Dislikes: Bumps and bruises
Bumps' besties:

RAYN	MELTSY	CRUMBLES

A Tidy Slidey Smashling

BUNKINS

BOING! BOING! Bunkins is a very bouncy Bunneroo Smashling that loves playing games, especially hide-and-seek. The funny thing is, fidgety Bunkins cannot keep still and is easily found when hiding.

FUN FACT

Bunneroos poop out jelly beans, but you wouldn't want to eat them! And when Bunneroos turn into Bashlings, something quite awful happens, making their poop very eggy indeed!

About: Bouncy, fast-talking, and confident
Rarity: Common
Likes: Playing hide-and-seek
Dislikes: Big meals
Bunkins' besties:

ELLA

GRUFF

CUDDLES

A Bunneroo Smashling

SERIES 2

DID YOU KNOW?

Bitter Bashlings often try to foil kind and caring Captain Buck's plans. There's always a sneaky Meañata that gets in the way of Buck's quests.

An Explorer Smashling

CAPTAIN BUCK

Ahoy there! What a Smashling Captain Buck is! Brave leader and epic adventurer, this intrepid explorer is always off in search of lost treasure, undiscovered artifacts, or secrets that lie hidden throughout the Piñataverse.

About: Bold, brave, and caring
Rarity: Uncommon
Likes: Adventures
Dislikes: Not having a plan

Captain Buck's besties:

WIGGLES	NOAKS	CONKS

56

CHA CHA

TICK! TICK! KABOOM! Bursting onto many a Piñataverse scene, Cha Cha is an entertaining thrill-seeker. Making trick-shot videos with its besties for their Smashling TV show keeps this Kaboom Smashling happy. You can guarantee an elaborate ending to each and every episode . . . usually some kind of explosion. With that injection of action, it's no wonder the channel gets millions of views!

FUN FACT

Cha Cha is also known as Cha Cha Boom, the Boomster, and Cha Cha B.

WHOOPS!

This bombastic Cha Cha has exploded into a bitter Bashling. Can it transform back again?

About: Determined, smart, and funny
Rarity: Rare
Likes: Trick shots and its Smashling TV show
Dislikes: Waiting
Cha Cha's besties:

SOCKS	FRANKLIN	NELSON

A Kaboom Smashling

CHEEP CHEEP

Doesn't this little Smashling look cute? But beware, hiding behind all that sunshine-yellow fuzz is one rough, tough Fluffy Fluff! Don't worry too much, Cheep Cheep's toughness is saved purely for its tangles with Meañatas and Bashlings.

FUN FACT

Cheep Cheep's cheep is pretty gruff, too. It communicates in an ultra-deep voice—not like your usual high-pitched birdsong.

About: Rough, tough, and buff
Rarity: Common
Likes: Arm wrestling
Dislikes: Meañatas and Bashlings
Cheep Cheep's besties:

LOU LOU	DRAKE	BEEP BOOP

A Fluffy Fluff Smashling

FUN FACT

Duckityboo feathers are the softest objects known to any Smashling, even softer than the softest of marshmallow snow that covers the Marshmallow Mountains. The feathers smell like blueberry pancakes. This is delightful until the aroma makes you sneeze. Once you start, you won't be able to sto . . . **ACHOO!**

CHERRY BLOOM

An extremely rare and highly prized Smashling, Cherry Bloom is very playful and lively. Cherry Bloom has a natural talent for throwing the best parties, which often end up in epic pillow fights with duckityboo feathers flying everywhere! The neat Cherry Bloom can't stand mess though, so its lively parties are often followed by marathon cleaning sessions!

About: Bright, tidy, and juicy
Rarity: Epic
Likes: Pillow fights
Dislikes: Mess

Cherry Bloom's besties:

COLIN	BERRY BOO	KEE WEE

A Berry Bling Smashling

CHERRY BUN

An absolute treat for you to meet, Cherry Bun is a ton of fun with frosting and a cherry on top! This disco-loving Smashling rocks the floor with its fabulous floss and can dance non-stop, bringing all the sweet moves to the party.

DID YOU KNOW?

This Floss Frost Smashling's favorite hangout is the water park. It hates getting soggy, but there's an awesome dance floor and it's a favorite haunt for all its fantastic friends, too.

A Floss Frost Smashling

About: Spirited, sweet, and sassy
Rarity: Common
Likes: Flossing
Dislikes: A slippery dance floor

Cherry Bun's besties:

BLOOPY	GUS	SWIRLY WURL

FUN FACT

Climb Bear Smashlings only eat candalyptus leaves. Candalyptus is a special kind of candy plant that only grows in the Rumble Jungle.

CHEWY

Curious Chewy is a clumsy Smashling who loves investigating. Sadly, it's often tricked by sneaky bitter Bashlings pretending to be helpful Smashlings. Chewy ends up falling into trouble, sometimes quite literally, and is oblivious to danger. But fear not! Lovable Chewy's cheeriness means that things always work out well for this cuddly Climb Bear Smashling . . . in the end.

Chewy's besties:

DASH	TUTTI BEL	GARBY

About: Happy, easy-going, and secretly determined
Rarity: Rare
Likes: Climbing and sleeping (not at the same time)
Dislikes: A varied diet

WHOOPS!

It appears Chewy has been tricked by a sneaky Bashling once again!

A Climb Bear Smashling

FUN FACT

The majority of the Piñata Village was built by Chuck!

CHUCK

So, how much wood would Chuck chuck if Chuck could chuck wood? Phew! Try saying that three times super fast! Chuck actually does throw wood all day, every day, and there is far too much wood to count. In fact, Toothy Nibblers are famous for making almost anything out of wood, and Chuck uses the wood it collects to build the most beautifully constructed dams along the Rainbow River.

Chuck's besties:

FERN	LEAKY	POCA JO JO

About: Busy, creative, and driven
Rarity: Common
Likes: Construction
Dislikes: The Dam Crushers

DID YOU KNOW?

A group of bitter Bashlings called the Dam Crushers was formed with the sole purpose of breaking Chuck's dams. Luckily, Toothy Nibblers have quite a bite, so these bitter Bashlings can be easily scared off with a toothy grin.

SPLASH!

FUN FACT

Sunshine provides Smashlings with vitamins that enrich their skin. Many Bashlings are deficient in vitamins due to a lack of sunlight in the Swamplands, oh . . . and wearing big hoods.

COLIN

CANNONBALL! This Totally Tropical Smashling loves a splashing Piñata pool party, especially one with diving and jumping into the water. After a quick dip, cool dude Colin enjoys lying in the sun poolside. Colin always slaps on some Smashling sunscreen for protection from the Piñata sunrays.

About: Smiley, funny, and cool
Rarity: Rare
Likes: A quick dip in the pool
Dislikes: Pizza
Colin's besties:

BERRY BOO	KEE WEE	CHERRY BLOOM

WHOOPS!

Looks like Colin has been turned into a Bashling! Here's hoping Berry Boo, Kee Wee, and Cherry Bloom can lure it to the Rainbow River to make it sweet again.

HEE! HEE! HEE!

A Totally Tropical Smashling

DID YOU KNOW?

Sometimes Conks can be found bathing in Rainbow River. The water dries, hardens, and regenerates this Smashling's skin, doing wonders!

CONKS

You may be able to spot Conks hanging out in the treetops, but it takes a keen eye to find this cunning camouflage expert. The Clonky Donk Smashling waits patiently for the perfect moment to let go of branches and land on the heads of unsuspecting Meañatas and Bashlings. It then races off and hides from the dazed and confused meanies once again. **Ha! Ha! Ha!**

About: Stealthy, quick, and tactical
Rarity: Common
Likes: Falling from trees
Dislikes: Meañatas and Bashlings

Conks' besties:

WIGGLES

NOAKS

CAPTAIN BUCK

CRUMBLES

Crumbles is an impeccable perfectionist. This Neaty Treat Smashling doesn't like **ANYONE** touching its bow tie. It spends hours in front of the mirror making sure it's straight. Crumbles likes be up in the Marshmallow Mountains, lounging in the snow, sipping on a glass of cold marzimoo milk, and looking in icy reflections to check on its perfectly-aligned bow tie.

FUN FACT

There was a time when bitter Bashlings saw Crumbles as a soft target, and they would sneak up and try to tug its bow tie. But since Crumbles took a Bashling by surprise by scattering sprinkles everywhere and chasing it away, Bashlings are more cautious to mess with its beloved bow tie.

A Neaty Treat Smashling

About: Particular, precise, and perfectionist
Rarity: Uncommon
Likes: Collecting bow ties
Dislikes: A hot oven

Crumbles' besties:

RAYN

BUMPS

MELTSY

SERIES 1

DID YOU KNOW?
Cuddles loves the local wildlife and looks after the orchards of Candy Apple Trees. Although Cuddles snacks on the gooey caramel, it never takes more than it needs.

CUDDLES

Hungry Dare Bear Smashlings adore eating from Candy Apple Trees. But they must bee-ware not to disturb the fiercely-protective, stingy, wingy, buzzing Candy Bees. These critters have a nasty sting and do not care to share with a Dare Bear. It's a beary good thing that Cuddles happens to be an expert Caramel Sap collector.

About: Daring, hungry, and cuddly
Rarity: Common
Likes: Caramel candies
Dislikes: Bee stings

Cuddles' besties:

BUNKINS	GRUFF	ELLA

A Dare Bear Smashling

`66

VISIT THE WATER WOWLER AT THE MECHA ZONE WATER PARK

FUN FACT

Dash loves to race, but hates traffic! That's why Dash prefers to run everywhere rather than ride in a car or train.

DASH

Don't be surprised if you miss this super-fast Smashling hurtling around! Hyper-competitive, energetic, and lively, Dash is always looking for a race and turns everything into a competition. This ambitious Frizz Fuzz always wants to win and be the center of attention. Optimistic Dash doesn't understand other Smashlings that aren't as competitive, and gets easily upset when they don't want to race.

About: Motivated, competitive, and energetic
Rarity: Common
Likes: Racing
Dislikes: Traffic jams

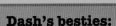

Dash's besties:

CHEWY	TUTTI BEL	GARBY

A Frizz Fuzz Smashling

DEARIE

This Munch Crunch Smashling is the minder and coach driver for the famous opera singer Gribby. Dearie adores its best friend, but secretly hates opera and sneaks off for a drink of giggle juice with Shivers while Gribby is performing.

DID YOU KNOW? Dearie has a huge appetite and will never miss an after-show buffet.

Dearie's besties:

GRIBBY SHIVERS DORIS

About: Proud, loyal, and friendly
Rarity: Rare
Likes: A buffet
Dislikes: Opera

A Munch Crunch Smashling

A Crafty Crocodillo Smashling

SERIES 1

DORIS

Doris loves the theater, especially the opera, which makes this Crafty Crocodillo perfect as the manager of operatic superstar Gribby. Doris sneaks Smashlings backstage to meet Gribby, for a fee of course! Doris also runs the Gribby Fan Club, where they sell merch and signed posters.

About: Organized, crafty, and resourceful
Rarity: Common
Likes: The theater and the opera
Dislikes: Waiting in long lines

DID YOU KNOW?

Doris once tried to sing opera itself, but the crowd threw some Duckityboo feathers at it! That wasn't very nice!

Doris's besties:

SHIVERS	GRIBBY	DEARIE

FUN FACT

Drake is in search of the most valuable record of all time, Planet Piñata by The Smashling Spin Wonders.

About: Ambitious, creative, and fast-talking
Rarity: Common
Likes: Vintage vinyl
Dislikes: Losing keys

Drake's besties:

CHEEP CHEEP BEEP BOOP LOU LOU

DRAKE

This Hiphopper Potter Mouse Smashling has huge ambitions of one day becoming a superstar rapper and building a clothing brand. Drake loves a bargain and likes spending time around the Piñata Village shops looking for vintage music records and inspiration.

WHOOPS!

Drake has accidentally hiphopped its way into becoming a grumpy Bashling. Hopefully, Drake will transform back soon to fulfill its dreams of stardom.

A Hiphopper Potter Mouse Smashling

71

FUN FACT

This Wet Weather Smashling loves a board game and is extremely competitive at Snakes and Ladders.

DROPLET

PITTER, PATTER, PITTER, PATTER. Droplet can be a bit blue at times and is often seen as a doomy gloomy Smashling. But it is fiercely loyal and always quick to help protect and give thoughtful opinions to friends.

A Wet Weather Smashling

About: Caring, doubting, and rainy
Rarity: Common
Likes: Board games
Dislikes: Damp, smelly socks

Droplet's besties:

RAY   PRICKLES   PATSY

DUSTY

Ready to hang out with this daring Dinky Cling? Dusty may be cute and friendly, but don't get on the wrong side of this smart Smashling, for it can be a formidable opponent when provoked. Dusty is agile and smart and has great strength for a Smashling.

DID YOU KNOW?

Dusty is always on the lookout for sneaky bitter Bashlings up to no good. So watch out, troublemakers!

About: Bold, smart, and loving
Rarity: Rare
Likes: Hanging out
Dislikes: Bullies

Dusty's besties:

RUS	MARSH	FANKLE

A Dinky Cling Smashling

A Happy Yup Pup Smashling

ELLA

You'll be grinning from ear to ear if you happen to come across a Happy Yup Pup Smashling—their smiles are totally infectious! With a love for the finer things in life, Ella has a very large collection of plastic jewelry. This glamorous Smashling's prized possession is an exquisite ring embedded with a rather large plastic pink gem. And yes, you'd be correct in thinking that the gem perfectly matches its adorable head bow. But of course it does, darling!

About: Glitzy, happy, and sophisticated
Rarity: Common
Likes: The finest and most expensive plastic jewelry
Dislikes: Early mornings
Ella's besties:

BUNKINS	CUDDLES	GRUFF

FUN FACT
There are rumors that Happy Yup Pup Smashlings can even make a Bashling smile for a second or two.

FUN FACT

El Grande Poco set up the SWF—the Smashling Wrestling Federation—with its besties OMG, Splats, and Fluffs, who are also amazing wrestlers. This organization packs out the Mecha Zone Wrestling Stadium every Saturday night.

EL GRANDE POCO

This brave wrestling Whizz Whirl is always hiding in bushes, pouncing out on unsuspecting Meañatas. It has even wrestled a few to the floor! That's why El Grande Poco is hailed a hero across the Piñataverse! A small Smashling with a huge personality, Poco's pride and joy is its rather large collection of wrestling belts, which are displayed in the foyer of the Mecha Zone Wrestling Stadium.

About: Confident, strong, and loyal
Rarity: Common
Likes: Its wrestling belt collection
Dislikes: Chafing thighs
El Grande Poco's besties:

OMG	SPLATS	FLUFFS

A Whizz Whirl Smashling

About: Kind, strong, and adventurous
Rarity: Uncommon
Likes: A decent hair conditioner
Dislikes: Tourists

FANKLE

Nature-loving Fankle enjoys the great outdoors and exploring the Marshmallow Mountains. This Wild Woolyup loves knitwear, and its wooly style is talked about all over the Piñataverse.

FUN FACT

An avid hiker, Fankle has been known to wander 500 miles or more!

Fankle's besties:

PIP	DUSTY	MARSH

DID YOU KNOW?

Biggyboggybongo bushes thrive in marshy areas with a bit of sunlight. They expand when waterlogged and make bongo sounds when it rains heavily.

FERN

Chatterbox Fern can mostly be found bouncing around along the Rainbow River, chit-chatting away to Chuck. Fern's scintillating subject matters include how much Rainbow Water a Biggyboggybongo bush needs and questions like, "Do you think the Rainbow Whale eats clouds for food?" Chuck does really enjoy Fern's company, but is often too busy beavering away to contribute much.

About: Vibrant, lush, and resilient
Rarity: Uncommon
Likes: A chat
Dislikes: Wrinkled fingers and toes from being in the Rainbow River too long

Fern's besties:

CHUCK LEAKY POCA JO JO

A Leafy Shrubby Dub Smashling

A Skooshy Woosh Smashling

FUN FACT

Fizz Pop has been known to put whoopee cushions on Piñatas' seats and fake dog poo on the buffet table!

DID YOU KNOW?

Some Smashlings have tried to contain this lively little Skooshy Woosh but find that it's much easier to just enjoy the pranks and laugh along.

FIZZ POP

You'd better have your wits about you when Fizz Pop's in town. Infamous for causing complete chaos at every celebration, this Skooshy Woosh Smashling is a bit of a rascal. With its habit of loudly exploding with excitement after a prank, you can usually tell when Fizz Pop has been up to its old tricks again.

Fizz Pop's besties:

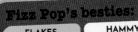

FLAKES   HAMMY   SPRINKLES

About: Energetic, excitable, and mischievous
Rarity: Uncommon
Likes: Pranks
Dislikes: Sitting still

OOPS!

DID YOU KNOW?
Flakes' favorite TV show is Game of Cones.

FLAKES

Hardworking Flakes worries **A LOT.** Quick to panic, this wired Melty Welty can end up in a sticky puddle of its own making. Flakes is very friendly and loves hanging out with its buddies in its extremely clean and tidy home. With its more optimistic personality, Fizz Pop, one of Flakes' closest friends, encourages the Melty Welty perfectionist not to worry so much, and even brings it out of its cone on occasion.

About: Polite, generous, and anxious
Rarity: Common
Likes: Being with friends
Dislikes: Being rushed
Flakes' besties:

HAMMY	FIZZ POP	SPRINKLES

A Melty Welty Smashling

FLUFFS

Fluffs may look like a cute and cuddly llama, but this tough Nimble Wimbler has stood its ground to more Meañatas than any other Smashling! Bashlings have certainly learned to avoid Fluffs, who is a member of the SWF (Smashling Wrestling Federation). To relax after a good wrestle, Fluffs likes lying in a floatation tank. In fact, it's the only way to calm Fluffs down.

DID YOU KNOW?

Fluffs' hero move is called "The Alpaca Punch." It leaves Bashlings stunned for days.

A Nimble Wimbler Smashling

About: Tough, rough, and gruff
Rarity: Rare
Likes: Flotation tanks
Dislikes: Bashlings and bling

Fluffs' besties:

EL GRANDE POCO

OMG

SPLATS

FRANKLIN

Let's go, Franklin! Totally dominating the basketball trick-shot scene with its bouncy, energetic style, Franklin is the life of the party on Smashling TV's hit show. Alongside its bestie, Cha Cha, who runs the show, Franklin consistently racks up millions of views. Always crushing it out on court, this Scoopy Hoop Smashling is number one and all about having fun!

About: Bouncy, lively, and fun
Rarity: Common
Likes: Slam dunks and 3-pointers
Dislikes: Punctures
Franklin's besties:

 CHA CHA

NELSON

SOCKS

A Scoopy Hoop Smashling

WHOOPS!

Yikes! Looks like Franklin dribbled and bounced into the path of a Meañata and was turned into a Bashling! Hopefully it'll slam dunk its way out of the Swamplands and back on to the basketball scene soon.

DID YOU KNOW?

After Garby mistakenly got in the wrong line at the Smashling Software Center, it had its circuit board upgraded with a super smart computer! Garby thought it was in the line for waste and recycling removal.

GARBY

This Dumpster Trunk Smashling is a one-robot clean-up team that munches its way through leftovers, litter, and generally anything lying around. It's great for the environment, but honestly, Garby is just a really hungry Smashling.

About: Logical, calculated, and hungry
Rarity: Common
Likes: Eating trash
Dislikes: Hair clips (they get caught in its teeth)

A Dumpster Trunk Smashling

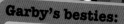

Garby's besties:

CHEWY	DASH	TUTTI BEL

FUN FACT

Bubble balloon bushes are extraordinary! The bushes have bubble balloon leaves that pump up before your eyes, only to dramatically pop on the thorns of the vines on the same bush. Then the process happens all over again.

DID YOU KNOW?

Giggles has an unusual and contagious laugh that will turn a grumpy day into the best day ever!

GIGGLES

Giggles by name, giggles by nature! This fizzy Giggly Wiggler just cannot stop laughing. Well, you would certainly chuckle, too, if you were full of sparkly bubbles fizzing up and down your insides. Giggles once completely lost its lid while playing in the Piñata Village and its bubbles went flat. Friends rallied around to cheer Giggles up, but it was no use. Luckily, they found the lid under a bubble balloon bush, and after a bit of jiggling, the lid was back in place. Giggles soon fizzed up and got its laughter going again.

About: Bubbly, happy, and giggly
Rarity: Rare
Likes: Giggling
Dislikes: Losing its lid
Giggles' besties:

LOLLY

LOL

SLURPY

A Giggly Wiggler Smashling

GRIBBY

Everyone in the Piñata Village is croaking on about this classically trained opera singer. Actually, Gribby once lost its croak and had to visit the Center for Injured Smashlings, where the Gobby Frogger was nursed back to health. Luckily, they keep spare "croaks" in jars locked in the storeroom. Wealthy Gribby now gives generous donations to support the Center.

A Gobby Frogger Smashling

About: Sophisticated, pompous, and generous
Rarity: Common
Likes: Opera
Dislikes: Pop culture

Gribby's besties:

SHIVERS

DEARIE

DORIS

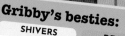

WHOOPS!

Gribby appears to have fallen from operatic stardom to the depths of grumpy star-gloom as a bitter and bad underground Bashling. Let's hope its fans can cheer Gribby back to the stage.

GRUFF

Gruff is a typical Tufty Terrier Smashling that just cannot help but look out of the window and bark at passerby all day. The sad thing is, Gruff actually really loves having company, but its barking keeps visitors away. Gruff's favorite guest is Cuddles, who brings caramel cookies. It is very entertaining to watch Gruff try extra hard not to wolf down those treats!

DID YOU KNOW?

Behind its barking exterior, Gruff is a big softie, loves a good old back scratch, a cozy bed, and a cup of warm marzimoo milk at the end of the day.

About: Sociable, excitable, and loud
Rarity: Epic
Likes: Barking
Dislikes: Being alone

A Tufty Terrier Smashling

Gruff's besties:

BUNKINS | ELLA | CUDDLES

GUS

Too cool for a regular swimming pool, this extreme Gnarly-Whal Smashling loves performing expertly-executed water stunts at the Mecha Zone Water Park. Gus is a legendary somersaulting Smashling and a popular celebrity diver, drawing huge crowds from far and wide to witness its incredible take-offs, tucks, twists, and tricks!

FUN FACT

Gus holds a Piñataverse World Record for the highest dive known to Smashlings.

About: Popular, athletic, and stylish
Rarity: Legendary
Likes: Performing in front of large crowds
Dislikes: Going to the dentist
Gus' besties:

BLOB	BLOOPY	SHIVERS

A Gnarly-Whal Smashling

HAMMY

A bold and high-spirited Burgeroo, this saucy Smashling is hard-working, stopping at nothing to get the job well done. But it's not all hard work. To relax, Hammy loves watching cheesy movies and listening to cheesy music with friends, and generally having a cheesy ol' time.

About: Observant, strong-minded, and protective
Rarity: Epic
Likes: All things cheesy. Cheesy music, cheesy movies, saying cheese in cheesy photos, cheese on everything . . . but not smelly cheese . . . smelly cheese doesn't count, only burger cheese
Dislikes: Pickles

DID YOU KNOW?

Hammy loves cheese. If Hammy doesn't have cheese, it's known to get a bit saucy.

Hammy's besties:

FIZZ POP	SPRINKLES	FLAKES

A Burgeroo Smashling

HAZ

No Smashling knows what Haz really looks or sounds like, as the ultra-cautious Health and Safety Smashling never takes off its protective yellow suit. The suit protects Haz from one of the worst smells in the entire Piñataverse . . . Parpy. Parpy is actually Haz's best friend and WOAH, its smell can make your eyes water. Even bitter Bashlings have been known to faint from the fumes.

About: Cautious, clean, and safe
Rarity: Common
Likes: Health and safety
Dislikes: Germs

Haz's besties:

PARPY	ROYDON	SIX

HELPY

Car-sales Smashling Helpy is super-friendly and honest. This Data Whirr Smashling has been programmed to give accurate data to help the car dealership price their work and vehicles. The problem? Helpy isn't a great negotiator and is easily convinced to trade too cheaply. Bargain, anyone?

FUN FACT

A Wobbly Bobbly sandwich is a delicious snack you can find at Berry Boo's sandwich shop.

About: Easily led, gentle, and helpful
Rarity: Rare
Likes: Helping customers
Dislikes: Boarsy choking on Wobbly Bobbly sandwiches

Helpy's besties:

BOARSY

POOKS

TWIST

A Data Whirr Smashling

FUN FACT

Candythons are long running races, during which competitors eat a lot of delicious candy vegetables.

A Tri Horn Smashling

HERBY

Ewww! Herby is infamous for its mahoosive dino doo-doos! This Tri Horn eats lots of vegetables and drinks too much coffee, which keeps it regular. The super-fit Smashling loves running candython races, keeping Herby in incredible shape.

About: Generous, sporty, and jolly
Rarity: Epic
Likes: Leafy greens
Dislikes: Meteorites
Herby's besties:

KIKI	REGGIE	STEGGY

HONEY

When this determined Smashling burst out of its Rainbow Pod, it discovered it had landed in the middle of an enormous honey-flavored bush. *Sweeeet!* From that moment on, Honey was hooked on honey. This very hungry Claw Paw will let nothing come between it and food.

TIP

Always have a few pots of the sticky stuff ready when inviting this ferocious little Smashling to a party.

About: Hungry, determined, and unafraid
Rarity: Common
Likes: Honey
Dislikes: Strong-smelling perfumes

Honey's besties:

STIG   WAFFLES   RUFF

A Claw Paw Smashling

JASPER

Tiggler Smashlings sharpen their teeth by nibbling on caramel rocks that can be found on the banks of the Rainbow River. Delicious! Jasper is a big joker and loves being silly. In fact, Jasper doesn't take life too seriously at all, except when it comes to its roar. Despite its best efforts to be a ferocious Tiggler, Jasper's growl is more of a meow! It doesn't help that it has caramel permanently stuck in its teeth. Although Jasper lacks patience, we're sure that roar will eventually come.

About: Confident, silly, and loyal
Rarity: Uncommon
Likes: Caramel rocks
Dislikes: Not having a loud roar
Jasper's besties: Jet, Meow, and Laze

DID YOU KNOW?
Jasper is courageous when it needs to be and jumps in head-first to protect its friends.

FUN FACT
Jasper once roared really loudly in its sleep. Unfortunately, it didn't hear it!

MEOW

JET

LAZE

A Blueberry Bush Cub **Smashling**

JET

You could say Jet hit the ground running and hasn't looked back. Its Rainbow Pod sped through the skies as if it had jet engines and, just before hitting the ground, two blue legs poked out of the bottom and landed with expert control. This Blueberry Bush Cub is one epic scout that loves the outdoors and adventure. There is, however, one thing that turns a brave Blueberry Bush Cub into a shivering scaredy cat—the spiteful Glooms. Jet is terrified by their mere presence! Bashlings often try to sneak up on Jet and place a Gloom nearby.

About: Brave, adaptable, and inspiring
Rarity: Uncommon
Likes: Adventures
Dislikes: Glooms
Jet's besties: Meow, Laze, and Jasper

MEOW

FUN FACT

Glooms come from the Swamplands and are foolish and tricky, but not scary at all. However, Blueberry Bush Cubs are filled with fear if they spot one near them.

JASPER

LAZE

WHOOPS!

Distracted by a Gloom, Jet was captured and turned into a Bashling. Will this brave adventurer be rescued?

A Fuzzberry Smashling

DID YOU KNOW?

Kee Wee has a funny reaction to drinking marzimoo milk. Its face swells up until Kee Wee starts floating into the sky like a lost balloon. Fortunately, it's not painful and the swelling only lasts for a few minutes before slowly deflating and allowing Kee Wee to float back down to safety.

KEE WEE

Kee Wee has a furry, thin exterior and a soft, sweet center, making this Smashling incredibly kind and caring. Fuzzberry Smashlings always help others, whether they want help or not. Once, Kee Wee helped an elderly Piñata cross a busy main road in the Mecha Zone, but the Piñata didn't want to cross and got stuck on the other side of the road for an entire afternoon. It wasn't happy at all. As Kee Wee skipped off whistling, you could see the Piñata shake its stick in annoyance. This sort of occurrence happens daily. But at least Kee Wee's heart is in the right place.

About: Caring, kind-hearted, and helpful
Rarity: Legendary
Likes: Helping
Dislikes: Marzimoo milk

Kee Wee's besties:

BERRY BOO   CHERRY BLOOM   COLIN

DID YOU KNOW?

As much as Kiki loves playgrounds, merry-go-rounds are a no go! They make this blue dino turn as green as Herby after too many spins.

KIKI

Do you think it See Saur us? It sure did! This See Saur Smashling has exceptional eyesight and nothing goes unnoticed! Unsurprisingly, its favorite game to play with its besties is hide-and-seek, but it loves all games. You'll often find Kiki in the park or the playground, swinging on the swings or slipping down the slide. Have you ever seen a See Saur seesaw? It's quite a sight for See Saur eyes!

About: Youthful, perky, and playful
Rarity: Epic
Likes: Playgrounds
Dislikes: Grazed knees

Kiki's besties:

| REGGIE | STEGGY | HERBY |

A See Saur Smashling

FUN FACT

Bananoos are a nutritious soft candy treat found in the Piñataverse. A Mashorilla Smashling can eat up to fifty bananoos a day!

A Mashorilla Smashling

KNUCKLES

This knowledgeable Mashorilla is one of the smartest Smashlings in the whole Piñataverse. Knuckles tries to keep busy challenging other Smashlings to games of chess and eating many squishy bananoos, but still gets bored very easily. Openhearted and peace-loving, this clumsy Smashling got its name not from fighting but from knocking things over with its knuckles!

About: Talkative, wise, and playful
Rarity: Uncommon
Likes: Bananoos and playing chess
Dislikes: Boredom

Knuckles' besties:

ROLLY

RICHIE

SNOOTS

LAZE

Behold, Laze—faster than lightning, quicker than wind and . . . lazier than a lazy Sunday afternoon in lazy town! Blink and you might miss this superfast Sprintlet Smashling when it gets going, but this happens only once in a blue moon. The rest of the time, Laze can be found resting, sleeping, or lolling around the Piñata Village. Laze may be the fastest Smashling in the Piñataverse, but it is also the laziest.

About:
Non-competitive, honest, and chilled
Rarity: Uncommon
Likes: Resting
Dislikes: Blue moons

FUN FACT

Blue moons are very rare and unpredictable. The last Piñata blue moon happened only a few weeks ago, so no one is expecting another one any time soon.

DID YOU KNOW?

Dash is constantly asking Laze for a race, but Laze just can't be bothered, which infuriates Dash.

Laze's besties:

JASPER	JET	MEOW

A Sprintlet Smashling

WORKS

LEAKY

Meet Leaky, the Spray Candoo with a "can do" attitude and a head full of paint! Leaky loves nothing more than spraying the town red. This works out well because Leaky spends its time working alongside its best friend Chuck. As Chuck builds, Leaky spray-paints, and together they've created and decorated most of the buildings in the Piñata Village.

FUN FACT

This happy and positive Smashling's paint color is determined by the color of the bubbleberry juice it has drunk. The majority of the time, Leaky is full of red paint, as that is its favorite flavor.

Leaky's besties:

CHUCK

FERN

POCA JOJO

About: Artistic, upbeat, and hardworking
Rarity: Common
Likes: Red bubbleberry juice
Dislikes: Being shaken

A Spray Candoo Smashling

About: Happy, funny, and outgoing
Rarity: Common
Likes: Elaborate tricks and awards
Dislikes: Poorly organized events

LOL

Having a party? Need entertainment? Look no further than LOL! This awesome Smashling provides the **ULTIMATE** party packages. LOL is a massively happy Smashling and spends every waking hour laughing to itself as it thinks of new material for its shows. LOL's latest act is a wonderfully coordinated routine, supported by ten lively little gymnastic Looms that run on stage and hurl each other up into the air for LOL to elaborately juggle. It's incredibly funny and has the audience laughing out loud from start to finish.

FUN FACT

LOL hands out lots of lollipops at the end of a show, which is a joke as Piñatas think LOL's name means "Lots Of Lollipops". Everyone knows LOL stands for "Laugh Out Loud" . . . well, everyone except for Piñatas that is. LOL.

LOL's besties:

LOLLY	GIGGLES	SLURPY

An Entertainer Smashling

LOLLY

This Rainbow Drip Smashling is highly energetic and has a personality as bright as its colorful appearance. Lolly loves to hang out with its lively friends, but must be careful not to get too hot around the popsicle stick. **Lolly + heat = A messy, sticky rainbow puddle.** To cool down, Lolly likes to rest under the shade of a Piñata tree or take a nice freeze in an ice bath.

DID YOU KNOW?

Things tend to stick to Lolly, which can be annoying. Don't even mention the time Lolly fell over on gravel. There were bits stuck to poor Lolly for months!

Lolly's besties:

SLURPY	LOL	GIGGLES

About: Generous, bashful, and jolly
Rarity: Epic
Likes: Ice baths
Dislikes: Gravel

A Rainbow Drip Smashling

LOU LOU

With dreams of one day making it big as a solo superstar, Lou Lou currently sings backup for the HipHopper Potter Mouse Smashling Drake. This Sing Song Smashling is incredibly talented and very clever, too. Health-conscious Lou Lou is always drinking water, eating all its fruit and veggies, and getting lots of glorious sleep.

FUN FACT

Lou Lou hates bananoos because they give it really bad gas.

Lou Lou's besties:

DRAKE   CHEEP CHEEP   BEEP BOOP

About: Bubbly, outgoing, and lively
Rarity: Common
Likes: Singing
Dislikes: Bananoos

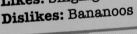

A Sing Song Smashling

MARSH

At first, the Unreasonable Snow Smashling was thought to be a myth, but actually it seemed to pop up all over the place in snowy areas. Rus, Dusty, and Fankle found this out as they trekked one day across the Marshmallow Mountains and heard a voice complaining about how hard it is to keep socks dry in the snow— it was Marsh the Unreasonable Snow Smashling! A snowball fight broke the ice, and they soon became best buddies.

FUN FACT

Marsh knows all the best snowboarding and ski routes across the snowy Marshmallow Mountains.

An Unreasonable Snow Smashling

Marsh's besties:

RUS	DUSTY	FANKLE

About: Active, disagreeable, and shy
Rarity: Common
Likes: Snowball fights
Dislikes: Bashlings

FUN FACT

Mellow runs a successful yoga practice with its besties, and its meditation retreats are hugely popular.

Mellow's besties:

MOONLET	WELLS	MINI BLUE

MELLOW

With a whole lotta heart, this Share Care Smashling gives the best big hugs and makes every Smashling feel loved and valued. AWWW! Calm and understanding, mellow Mellow is the perfect Smashling to have around when self-esteem is low. Everyone can do with a Mellow in their life!

About: Supportive, kind, and motivating
Rarity: Common
Likes: Beanbags and soft pillows
Dislikes: Heavily buttered sandwiches

A Share Care Smashling

MELTSY

Meltsy is a very mysterious Snow Smashling. It loves to create bizarre, sweet, icy treats that are a big hit throughout the Piñataverse. Meltsy mainly stays secluded in its hidden treat factory, camouflaged in the Marshmallow Mountains. The whole factory operation is organized and controlled by a curious little-known species of snow mushrooms called Snooms.

About: Imaginative, eccentric, and mysterious
Rarity: Common
Likes: Snowy innovation
Dislikes: Yellow snow

Meltsy's besties:

BUMPS	CRUMBLES	RAYN

A Snow Smashling

106

MELV

When Melv broke free of its Rainbow Pod, it exclaimed, "Well, is this it then?" in a downtrodden voice. Pip, Raskins, and Twinky, who found Melv, were shocked and speechless! Melv filled the silence with, "What time is lunch?" and "I expect there's nothing good to eat!" and slumped back into the shell of its pod. It turns out Melv is just a bit less optimistic compared to most Smashlings. But with the help of its besties, Melv has been able to reprogram some of its circuit boards to become much happier.

Melv's besties:

PIP	RASKINS	TWINKY

FUN FACT

Melv has a brain the size of the Piñata moon and takes great delight in solving "big brain" problems, such as helping Snoots to find its door key.

About: Intelligent, helpful, and downbeat
Rarity: Common
Likes: Big brain problems
Dislikes: Long walks

An Alley Chat Smashling

TIP

It's best not to stop Meow in the street for an autograph or you'll be there for hours, listening to the Alley Chat rattle on and on and on . . .

MEOW

Meow is a famous Alley Chat Smashling that talks non-stop. It's very rare for Meow to pause to catch its breath or cough up a fur ball. Yuck! This paw-some Smashling has a wildcat imagination and creates whimsical adventure stories about its pals Jasper, Jet, and Laze. Its whisker-twitching tales are legendary and have been published across the Piñataverse, making Meow a Smashling super-duper star.

Meow's besties:

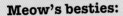

JASPER	JET	LAZE

About: Creative, imaginative, and chatty
Rarity: Common
Likes: Spinning a yarn
Dislikes: Fur balls

Mini Blue's besties:

MELLOW   MOONLET   WELLS

About: Intelligent, sensible, and chill
Rarity: Common
Likes: Spinning
Dislikes: Swampland pollution

MINI BLUE

This super-smart Wonder World Smashling has eleven PHB (Pretty Huge Brain) Candy Science qualifications. Amazed? Well, you should be. Mini Blue cares deeply about the environment. This Smashling spends most of its time researching the effects of the toxic pollution that creeps into the atmosphere from the Swamplands. It's seriously smelly stuff, but Mini Blue is still a pretty laid-back and happy Smashling that always makes time for parties and fun with friends.

A Wonder World Smashling

FUN FACT

Once, Moonlet fell asleep at a picnic party and Nelson the Moo Woo Smashling jumped over the sleepy Moonlet.

A Twinkler Smashling

MOONLET

Nocturnal Moonlet really comes alive at night. When every other Smashling is in the land of Nod, you'll see a sparkle of light at Moonlet's crib. This Twinkler Smashling has a **HUGE** appetite for midnight feasts, and as it digs into its snacks, you'll see its stars twinkle. Nice! Moonlet's snack of choice is mashed candicumbers spread on crackers. It often invites its best pals—Mini Blue, Mellow, and Wells—to partake in the treats. Which they do—as long as they can stay awake long enough!

Moonlet's besties:

MELLOW	MINI BLUE	WELLS

About: Hungry, generous, and nocturnal
Rarity: Common
Likes: Midnight snacks
Dislikes: Early mornings

NELSON

Be prepared to be amazed! As one of the biggest fans of Cha Cha's trick shots, Nelson soon befriended the Smashling through the comments section on one of the videos. Now they're best buddies, they hang out with Franklin and Socks, and they post lots of spectacular trick shots on the Smashlings TV channel.

FUN FACT

Nelson loves buying gifts, and most days there's some kind of interesting package turning up on the Smashling's porch.

About: Excitable, obliging, and generous
Rarity: Uncommon
Likes: Next-day deliveries
Dislikes: Slow Internet

A Moo Woo Smashling

Nelson's besties:

CHA CHA	FRANKLIN	SOCKS

NOAKS

Noaks has a big brain under all that shell. A quiet, logical thinker, this Fix Tink Smashling prefers the peaceful surroundings of its woodland workshop as it creates gadgets, fixes machines, and invents new and innovative products. Noaks always has a creative solution and is happiest spending its time tinkering away in solitude.

A Fix Tink Smashling

WIGGLES

DID YOU KNOW?

Noaks' inventions include a self-propelling wheelbarrow, a machine that collects candy from the woodland floor and turns it into candy butter (great on toast), and a high-speed miniature train line that Noaks uses to transport gadgets to and from the woodlands.

CAPTAIN BUCK

CONKS

About: Reserved, reliable, and resourceful
Rarity: Uncommon
Likes: Gadgets
Dislikes: Large crowds
Noaks' besties: Captain Buck, Conks, and Wiggles

DID YOU KNOW?
OMG's legendary signature move is the Elbow Gum Drop, which gets the fans screaming with excitement.

About: Strong, tough, and collaborative
Rarity: Uncommon
Likes: Elbow Gum Drops
Dislikes: Its original name

OMG's besties:

EL GRANDE POCO	FLUFFS	SPLATS

OMG

Slick OMG is the tag-team partner of the most famous wrestler in the Piñataverse—El Grande Poco. For many years, this Mucho Macho Smashling wrestled under its original name. Only once it changed its name to OMG did it become an ultra-famous Smashling, with fans chanting, **"YOU GO, OMG!"**

A Mucho Macho Smashling

STINKY FACT

Parpy's smell has even been known to make Bashlings faint!

About: Spritely, energetic, and smelly
Rarity: Common
Likes: Cutting the cheese
Dislikes: Sitting still for too long

PARPY

Parpy is a lively Smashling that is full of beans on many levels. As well as having some serious game on the basketball court, this Tinned Stinker also has some serious gas. This pro baller will never drop the ball, but constantly drops the stinkiest of foul smells that can clear a room quicker than a call for free Wobbly Bobbly sandwiches.

Parpy's besties:

HAZ   SIX   ROYDON

A Tinned Stinker Smashling

PATSY

Petal head-banging Patsy can be found rocking out to blast beats and power chords at metal concerts, jumping around and having fun with Ray, Prickles, and Droplet. Patsy can really rock hard and is completely energized with its friends around. Without them, Patsy would soon wilt after partying too hard for too long.

FUN FACT

Patsy's favorite band is Petallica— a powered-up flower metal rock band with loud drums that the crowd goes wild for.

About: Energetic, springy, and wild
Rarity: Common
Likes: Mosh pits
Dislikes: Wilting
Patsy's besties:

RAY	PRICKLES	DROPLET

A Metal Petal Smashling

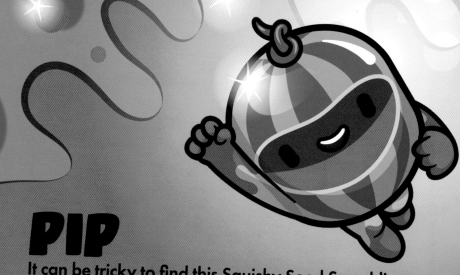

PIP

It can be tricky to find this Squishy Seed Smashling, as it's usually in the remotest parts of the Piñataverse perfecting some extreme sport or another! Pip loves biking down steep mountains, kayaking in the most dangerous parts of the Rainbow River, and even parachuting from The Giant Tree. Daring Pip only comes back to the mainland if it has an accident and needs to go to the Center for Injured Smashlings . . . or for parties, of course!

About: High-spirited, focused, and courageous
Rarity: Uncommon
Likes: Extreme sports
Dislikes: Being injured

Pip's besties:

DUSTY	MARSH	FANKLE

FUN FACT

Pip dreams of inventing a new extreme sport that Smashlings will play forever!

A Squishy Seed Smashling

DID YOU KNOW?

This Wide-Eyed Clamber Smashling just loves hanging out in the treetops with its besties. Fern talks enough for the whole group, which suits avid listener Poca Jo Jo just fine.

POCA JO JO

Poca Jo Jo is usually very shy and prefers to keep to itself and stay hidden high in the trees of the woodlands. But this Wide-Eyed Clamber Smashling does have a close-knit friend group with Chuck, Leaky, and Fern. At first, Poca Jo Jo just watched Chuck and Fern hang out around the banks of the Rainbow River, but it became fascinated with their marvelous constructions. Poca Jo Jo soon plucked up enough courage to come and say, "hey."

About: Quiet, reflective, and shy
Rarity: Common
Likes: Quiet time
Dislikes: Loud Smashlings

Poca Jo Jo's besties:

CHUCK   LEAKY   FERN

A Wide-Eyed Clamber Smashling

FUN FACT

Pooks won an award for the incredible design work it did on the Piñata Party Bus.

POOKS

Head on down to the car dealership and you'll find Pooks in the workshop, spraying up cars. This creative Graffosaurus Smashling can give any vehicle a funky and fresh new look. At the dealership, Helpy gives Pooks data reports on what has been sold. But the only font Helpy has in its system is Comic Sans, which Pooks not a fan of! So every time Pooks sees the reports it tries not to vomit.

A Graffosaurus Smashling

About: Focused, chill, and creative
Rarity: Epic
Likes: Car graphics
Dislikes: Comic Sans

Pooks' besties:

BOARSY

HELPY

TWIST

PRICKLES

Despite this little Wish Well Smashling's name and exterior, its personality is far from prickly. With a heart of gold, this shy, soft-natured soul loves nothing more than helping friends. The only issue is that Prickles' prickles can sometimes get in the way of group hugs. Ouch!

About: Organized, kind, and supportive
Rarity: Uncommon
Likes: Beach days in the sunshine and helping friends
Dislikes: Inflatables and loud noises

Prickles' besties:

| RAY | PATSY | DROPLET |

POP!

TIP

Avoid sudden loud noises around this lovable Smashling. Big bangs, pops, and crashes will send it running off to hide.

A Wish Well Smashling

PUGGSY

Don't let appearances deceive you with this little Chippy Whip! At first, Puggsy may look sweet and cute, but it is actually seriously yappy. It has scared many a Piñata in the past. But, fear not! It just takes some time to warm up to strangers.

TIP

If you take some time to get to know Puggsy, you'll soon be rewarded with the friendship of one of the most loyal Smashlings ever!

A Chippy Whip Smashling

Puggsy's besties:

SHAKEY	WIMBLY	SQUISH

About: Cautious, noisy, and lively
Rarity: Common
Likes: Cautiousness
Dislikes: Unfamiliar faces

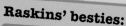

About: Playful, lively, and fun
Rarity: Common
Likes: Wheelbarrow rides
Dislikes: Large spoons

Raskins' besties:

PIP MELV TWINKY

RASKINS

If you love good-natured, hilarious pranks and tricks, then you'll very much enjoy the company of this Squish Squash Smashling scoundrel. Fall is the prime time for Raskins' rogue antics, so every Smashling in the Piñata Village keeps an eye out, making sure it isn't up to too much mischief.

FUN FACT

Raskins once bubble-wrapped the whole Piñata Village while everyone was asleep. What a popping party they had the next day!

WHOOPS!

Looks like the joke's on Raskins now—the trickster has been tricked into becoming a Bashling. Let's hope it can scamper out of this.

A Squish Squash Smashling

SERIES 2

FUN FACT

Ray always wears sunglasses and sunscreen to keep it safe from sunburn and eye damage.

RAY

Ray is always ready to share joy and happiness with everyone. Friendly, bubbly Ray chats with every Smashling it meets. This Sunshine Smashling's positivity is very infectious and rubs off on everyone—except Droplet, that is. Droplet is one of Ray's besties and can put a wet blanket on any exciting ideas Ray might have. Droplet usually has a good reason for its grumpiness, though. It's a great friend to Ray and just wants to keep its buddy safe.

A Sunshine Smashling

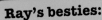

Ray's besties:

PRICKLES	PATSY	DROPLET

About: Positive, impulsive, and sociable
Rarity: Common
Likes: Mornings
Dislikes: Bedtime

RAYN

Oh deary me! Rayn can be a bit unsure of itself. One day, after visiting its bestie Meltsy, Rayn stumbled upon some glowing marshmallow moss on rocks high up in the Marshmallow Mountains. Feeling hungry (and unusually brave), Rayn ate some of the moss, and since then, this Smashling has the ability to fly for short periods of time.

NO ONE KNOWS . . .

Is marshmallow moss a rare Piñata plant? Or maybe it has something to do with the Snooms that have been mixing ice-treat ingredients together and forming something magical?

A Deary Me Smashling

About: Uncertain, unsuspecting, and gullible
Rarity: Common
Likes: Glowing marshmallow moss
Dislikes: Hard landings

Rayn's besties:

MELTSY	BUMPS	CRUMBLES

FUN FACT

Rumor has it that Reggie's legs actually move as quickly as its mouth.

A Dramasaur Smashling

REGGIE

Read all about it! Piñata Village drama follows Reggie wherever it goes! This Dramasaur Smashling loves nothing more than to babble away at high speed, sharing the latest and greatest gossip right as it unfolds. You can always rely on Reggie to spread the news and be on the go 24/7, speed-walking everywhere to bring you it all. Breaking news says that moving so fast is one of the reasons Reggie is so quick to find out what's going on around town.

About: Busy, dramatic, and informed
Rarity: Common
Likes: Speed-walking
Dislikes: Being kept out of the loop

Reggie's besties:

HERBY

KIKI

STEGGY

RICHIE

A bit of a perfectionist for pristine hair, Richie hates getting caught in the rain and getting all floofy. Being quite unlucky, this Roar Club Smashling always seems to get wet. Richie doesn't make a moaning, roaring fuss like most Roar Clubs, though. Richie has only ever roared once, and that was when it stepped in a splashy caramel puddle. Getting the fluffy Smashling's mane back to its former immaculate condition took a **roar**-fully long time.

About: Unlucky, neat, and stoic
Rarity: Uncommon
Likes: Having a tidy mane, pizza, and walking tours (not in the rain)
Dislikes: Getting wet

Richie's besties:

SNOOTS	ROLLY	KNUCKLES

FUN FACT

Richie's favorite food is pizza!

A Roar Club Smashling

ROLLY

Rolly is a super-kind, adorable, and very loving Pandoo Smashling that causes havoc by spinning and rolling around all over the place. It does come in handy when Bashlings are around, as this Pandoo Smashling will be ready to "strike" like a ten-pin bowling ball if challenged. Wwwwwheeeeeeeeeeeeeeeee!

About: Kind, smart, and cautious
Rarity: Uncommon
Likes: Rolling and more rolling
Dislikes: Waiting in line
Rolly's besties: Knuckles, Richie, and Snoots

KNUCKLES

RICHIE

SNOOTS

WARM HUGS

WHOOPS!
Oh dear, Rolly has turned into a Bashling and now rolling makes it feel giddy and sick. Maybe that's why it looks so green? Let's hope it changes back soon.

FUN FACT

Roydon is a massive basketball fan and hangs out courtside with its BFF, Six, the famous basketball player.

An Adventure Bot Smashling

ROYDON

Do you know the ultimate question that all Piñatas and Smashlings want to know the answer for? "Where does the Rainbow Whale come from?" Well, this Adventure Bot Smashling has been programmed to find out. The catch? If Roydon ever does find out, it won't be able to share the answer, as it hasn't been programmed to talk, and can only communicate in beeps and boops. **Beep! Beep! Boop!** What was that, Roydon? Hmm.

About: Daring, driven, and inquisitive
Rarity: Common
Likes: Mecha Zone Rockets basketball team
Dislikes: Low battery

Roydon's besties:

HAZ	PARPY	SIX

RUFF

This excitable Smashling loves splashing and jumping in caramel puddles along the banks of Caramel Lake. Ruff has so much fun glooping about with its pals that it never wants to go home, especially because that means big bubbly bath time, which is definitely not this Woofity Smashling's favorite activity.

A Woofity Smashling

DID YOU KNOW?

It takes a lot of coaxing and many belly rubs to encourage Ruff to take a bath.

About: Waggy, woofy, and playful
Rarity: Uncommon
Likes: Belly rubs
Dislikes: Bath time
Ruff's besties: Stig, Honey, and Waffles

FUN FACT

Ruff once jumped into a caramel puddle that was so deep it reached its nose. Ruff sneezed caramel bubbles for days after.

HONEY

WAFFLES

STIG

133

A Sticky Beak Smashling

RUS

Rus runs a blog, reporting on all the latest news happening across the Piñataverse. This Sticky Beak Smashling has sharp eyes and glides unnoticed above everyone's heads on the lookout for the latest scoop. When Rus isn't busy chasing leads, it explores the far reaches of the world. From the rolling hills to the dizzying heights of the Marshmallow Mountains, Rus has seen it all and always has a story to tell about its adventures.

DID YOU KNOW?

Despite Rus' exciting life, this Smashling loves to unwind with close friends Dusty, Fankle, and Marsh.

About: Inquisitive, observant, and adventurous
Rarity: Rare
Likes: A good scoop
Dislikes: An unpublished story
Rus' besties:

MARSH	DUSTY	FANKLE

FUN FACT

One of Shakey's movie reviews was so loved by the director, Shakey was invited to see the sequel's film set!

CINEVERSE

About: Intelligent, nervous, and humorous
Rarity: Uncommon
Likes: TV and film
Dislikes: Bright lights
Shakey's besties:

PUGGSY	WIMBLY	SQUISH

SHAKEY

Film buff Shakey loves watching movies, particularly old westerns. **Yee-haw!** Shakey's day job is writing film reviews for the website SMDb (Smashling Movie Database). The Pop Ping Smashling can be quite nervous, but relaxes watching comedy films with its besties. One day they all hope to make their very own movie together.

A Pop Ping Smashling

SHIVERS

You may hear Shivers telling tall tales about its adventures out on the Smashling Seas, but Shivers has never even left the Piñata Village! Maybe one day this Swimmy Tiddler will make its dreams come true.

DID YOU KNOW?

The younger Smashlings love to hear Shivers's stories. They know they aren't true, but that's the nice thing about fairytales.

A Swimmy Tiddler Smashling

About: Entertaining, imaginative, and persuasive
Rarity: Epic
Likes: Telling tall tales
Dislikes: Bigger fish in the sea
Shivers' besties:

GRIBBY	DEARIE	DORIS

About: Hard-working, serious, and a leader
Rarity: Common
Likes: Sponsorship deals
Dislikes: Itchy tracksuits
Six's besties:

HAZ	PARPY	ROYDON

FUN FACT

The Mecha Zone Rockets have had financial struggles over the last ten years and recently had a new investment from an unknown Smashling billionaire. It's all very exciting.

SIX

"Swish" Six takes its role as captain of the Mecha Zone Rockets basketball team very seriously. The team hasn't actually ever won a title, but Six is determined to dribble straight to the winning basket this season. Come on, you Rockets, it's time for a hot streak of three-pointers!

A Slam Dunk Smashling

A Burpy Wurpy Smashling

SLURPY

BURRRRPPPPPPP! That's right, everyone can hear this highly fizzed-up Burpy Wurpy's signature belch coming from miles around. Slurpy's famous belches have caused much laughter all over the Piñataverse. Some of the big ones can sound pretty disgusting, but as the belches actually scare away some of the nastiest Meañatas, they're a welcome sound to most Smashlings.

About: Cheerful, loud, and funny
Rarity: Uncommon
Likes: Rude noises
Dislikes: Wasps
Slurpy's besties: Lolly, LOL, and Giggles

LOL

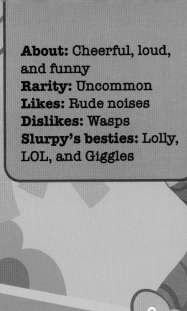

GIGGLES

LOLLY

FUN FACT

Slurpy holds the Smashling World Record for the longest and loudest belch. Nice!

BURRRRPPPPPP!

SNOOTS

As an extremely talented musician, Snoots plays just about every instrument known to Smashlings. The problem is the Tooty Toot Smashling can't remember where it's supposed to perform. Lucky for its fans, Snoots never forgets a tune once it's on stage!

DID YOU KNOW?

Snoots once crashed an opera performance by Gribby, and the two jammed on stage for hours.

A Tooty Toot Smashling

Snoots' besties:

ROLLY

KNUCKLES

RICHIE

About: Forgetful, indecisive, and musical
Rarity: Epic
Likes: Saxophone solos
Dislikes: Martial arts

An Inflate-a-ball Smashling

DID YOU KNOW?
Socks' positive self-talk tip is to praise yourself every day for something you've achieved.

SOCKS

Hyper-competitive Socks helps Cha Cha film trick-shot videos for the super-popular Smashlings TV channel. Always striving for the best and scared of making any mistakes, this Inflate-a-ball Smashling occasionally finds things get a bit much. But when anxiety takes its toll, Socks gives itself praise and a good, positive self-talk to help it stay focused and relaxed.

About: Competitive, fussy, and anxious
Rarity: Common
Likes: Positive vibes
Dislikes: Messing up
Socks' besties:

CHA CHA   FRANKLIN   NELSON

Splats' besties:

EL GRANDE POCO

OMG

FLUFFS

About: Strong, messy, and determined
Rarity: Common
Likes: Eating and wrestling
Dislikes: Being hungry

DID YOU KNOW?

Splats always has its headphones on to avoid hearing its own stomach rumbles.

SPLATS

Splats is a messy eater and big in the wrestling scene. It's a messy affair to wrestle and eat at the same time—something that Splats tends to do, as this hungry wrestler never seems to get full. The Belly Rumbler is one of Splats' renowned wrestling moves. It consists of a thunderous stomach growl as Splats launches itself off the top ropes while eating a Wobbly Bobbly sandwich before landing on its opponent.

A Rumbler Smashling

SPRINKLES

This Nutty Doh Smashling certainly sprinkles a lot of color all over Piñata Village. You never quite know what Sprinkles is going to do next, but the zany Smashling is so much fun to be around. Life is one huge adventure full of custard baths, jelly juggling, and chasing after wandering Looms.

A Nutty Doh Smashling

About: Colorful, talkative, and eccentric
Rarity: Legendary
Likes: A sprinkle fight
Dislikes: Marzipan
Sprinkles' besties:

HAMMY	FIZZ POP	FLAKES

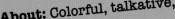

FUN FACT

Looms are red mushrooms that wander all over the forest. These fun guys enjoy a prank or two!

About: Unreserved, precious, and squeaky
Rarity: Rare
Likes: Digging and dress-up
Dislikes: Sharing its outfits
Squeak's besties:

BLUSH

STING

TUTAN

DID YOU KNOW?

Squeak will bury its favorite outfits in the dirt. Other Smashlings can't understand why it doesn't use the empty closet.

A Barky Warky Smashling

SQUEAK

Piñatas and Smashlings are always super-excited for new Smashlings to burst from their Rainbow Pods. When Squeak burst out, they thought it seemed to be a bit of a grumpy Barky Warky Smashling. But as soon as it opened its mouth, rather than a loud bark, a lovely little squeak came out. Adorable! Squeak's favorite place is Tutan's shop.

SQUISH

BOO! Made you jump! This Jammy Hodge-podger Smashling loves nothing more than doing just that. Squish's number-one activity is making Shakey laugh, either with a joke or by jumping out on Shakey when it least expects it. When Shakey hosts movie night, you can be sure that Squish will be there—and might bring few whoopee cushions, too!

BOO!

A Jammy Hodge-podger Smashling

About: Funny, bold, and mischievous
Rarity: Legendary
Likes: Scary movies
Dislikes: Rom coms
Squish's besties:

SHAKEY | PUGGSY | WIMBLY

DID YOU KNOW?

Squish loves a scary horror flick on movie night. Shakey's not as big a fan and sometimes has to hide behind Squish's jar lid!

FUN FACT

Steggy's favorite thing to chew is bubble gum, but it will never say no to a lollipop, either!

About: Daring, fun, and adventurous
Rarity: Common
Likes: Bubble gum
Dislikes: Heights

Steggy's besties:

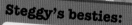

KIKI	REGGIE	HERBY

STEGGY

Roar-some Bubblesaurus Steggy loves blowing big bubblegum bubbles and has a Smashling World Record for the largest bubble. It was so large, Steggy actually took off with it and ended up floating high up into The Great Tree—higher than any Smashling has ever been (which was still only about halfway). The bubble did finally burst, and luckily the Rainbow Whale was flying past and managed to catch Steggy safely on its back. Steggy did end up with a rather dino-sore behind though.

A Bubblesaurus Smashling

About: Muddy, cheerful, and wild
Rarity: Rare
Likes: Caramel mud puddle parties
Dislikes: Broccoli

Stig's besties:

HONEY	WAFFLES	RUFF

DID YOU KNOW?

Caramel mud puddles aren't every Smashling's favorite thing, but they are Stig's!

A Thuddy Mud Smashling

STIG

This merry Smashling is definitely no stig in the mud, but it certainly likes to party in it. Stig's absolute favorite thing to do is wallow in mud in the gloopy areas around Lake Caramel with its pals. Sounds mucky and yucky, but some little Smashlings love nothing more than a caramel mud puddle party.

STING

Sting is a plugged-in and fully charged Flutter Flash Smashling that loves throwing electric shapes on the dance floor. On Wednesday nights, Sting teaches breakdance classes at the Electric Avenue dance studio. Sting has two signature dance moves—the Thunder Blunder, which is pretty fast and impossible to imitate, and the Electric Boogaloo, which is an ancient dance move that Sting has made popular again.

About: Truthful, humorous, and sparky
Rarity: Uncommon
Likes: Dancing to electric beats
Dislikes: Power cuts

Watch out! Think twice if Sting offers to shake your hand. His handshakes are, quite literally, shocking.

Sting's besties:

BLUSH

TUTAN

SQUEAK

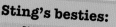

A Flutter Flash Smashling

149

Swirly Wurl's besties:

BLOOPY CHERRY BLOOM GUS

About: Consistent, creative, and perfectionist
Rarity: Rare
Likes: The Great Smashling Bake-Off
Dislikes: A burned bottom (on its cakes)

A Cup Cake Smashling

SWIRLY WURL

Knead-less to say, soft-peaked Swirly Wurl can mostly be found baking and selling cakes at the water park. Its cakes are legendary—light and fluffy, just like Swirly Wurl itself. This Cup Cake Smashling dreams of one day baking the largest cake the Piñataverse has ever seen, with a chocolate sponge covered in frosting, sprinkles, and edible glitter. Imagine a cake so big that you could cut out a door with rooms and live in it for an entire year . . . or at least until the sponge goes stale.

TUTAN

Tutan's fancy clothing shop is super popular when there's a party, and there's always a party in the Piñataverse! It gets so busy you can only visit the little Fair Oh-Me-Oh-My Smashling's shop if you have an appointment. With a horn on the front door, you have to toot-and-come-in! Sorry, Tutan, you may not like bad jokes, but that one was too hard to resist.

Tutan's besties:

BLUSH	STING	SQUEAK

DID YOU KNOW?
Tutan loves to dress up, but its regular wear isn't a costume.

About: Glitzy, chatty, and extroverted
Rarity: Uncommon
Likes: Sparkly jackets
Dislikes: Bad jokes

TUTAN'S

TOOT TOOT!

A Fair Oh-Me-Oh-My Smashling

TUTTI BEL

There's so much sweetness packed into this Prancer Smashling it makes your teeth hurt. On a cuteness scale of one to ten, Tutti Bel would be an eleven. This Prancer Smashling is not only adorable but it's also packed full of energy. Bouncing, skipping, and hopping everywhere, its energy lifts its friends when they're discouraged. There's never a dull moment with Tutti Bel around.

A Prancer Smashling

CHEWY

DASH

GARBY

FUN FACT

Tutti Bel loves hula-hooping. It formed a hula-hoop club that meets every Tuesday, called the Hooplets.

About: Extroverted, energetic, and empathetic
Rarity: Uncommon
Likes: Hula-hooping
Dislikes: Hiccups
Tutti Bel's besties: Chewy, Dash, and Garby

153

DID YOU KNOW?
As its batteries start to drain, Twinky gets tired and becomes much less competitive!

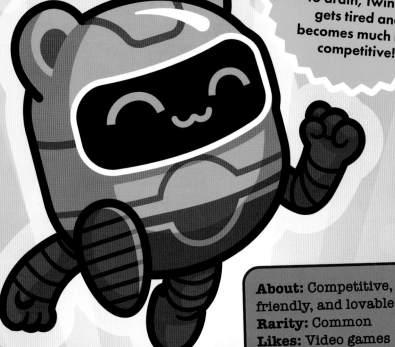

A Gamer Bot Smashling

About: Competitive, friendly, and lovable
Rarity: Common
Likes: Video games
Dislikes: Updating software and losing

TWINKY

If you never wanted to leave the house, Twinky has everything a Smashling could ever need: a built-in drinks machine, snack dispenser, fridge, microwave, and a games cartridge with all of the latest top game releases. Every Smashling loves having Twinky around, although the Gamer Bot is ultra-competitive, hates losing, and can play games for hours.

Twinky's besties:

PIP	MELV	RASKINS

TWIST

An absolute wiz at making and mending, Twist works with Pooks and Helpy at the car dealership. The Clunky Clunk Smashling converted an old bath into the fastest hot rod the Piñataverse has ever seen. Even better than that, Twist won a Choccy Woccy Wee Woo bar from Pooks, who said it couldn't be done. As well as working on cars, Twist loves the thrill of driving them and races in the Piñatona 500—the most prestigious race in the land!

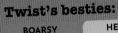

About: Organized, inventive, and thrill-seeking
Rarity: Common
Likes: Fixing things and racing bathtubs
Dislikes: Wearing stiff clothes

Twist's besties:

BOARSY	HELPY	POOKS

FUN FACT

Choccy Woccy Wee Woo bars are made by Berry Boo. The secret recipe is kept in a safe at the sandwich shop.

A Clunky Clunk Smashling

Waffles' besties:

STIG

HONEY

RUFF

About: Popular, aerobic, and entertaining
Rarity: Uncommon
Likes: Chocolate fountains
Dislikes: Belly flops

DID YOU KNOW?

At the end of each dive, Waffles loves to share the delicious treats that it has collected from the fountain, often sprinkled with extra chocolate and a dollop of whipped cream to taste.

WAFFLES

Waffles is an exclusive Scrummy Yummy Smashling who has made quite a name for itself in the Piñataverse. This popular waffle is known for its incredible dives into the chocolate fountain, which draws a crowd of Smashlings from all over the Piñataverse. The events are always filled with excitement and laughter, and Waffles is beloved by all who attend.

A Scrummy Yummy Smashling

WELLS

Wells is a very elusive Smashling who only shows up in Root Village every once in a while to hang out with its besties. Rumor has it that Wells has built a spaceship powered by astral dust and space rainbows, which this Galactic Maverick Smashling uses to zip around between planets.

About: Clever, mysterious, and elusive
Rarity: Rare
Likes: Space travel
Dislikes: Colds

A Galactic Maverick Smashling

FUN FACT

The Sticky Beak Smashling Rus wrote an article about Wells' adventures. It claimed that Wells has a secret hideout deep in the desert called "Area 59," but no one knows if this is true or not!

Wells' besties:

MELLOW	MOONLET	MINI BLUE

157

Wiggles' besties:

CAPTAIN BUCK	NOAKS	CONKS

A Wise-woo Smashling

About: Outspoken, sensitive, and clever
Rarity: Common
Likes: Peace and quiet
Dislikes: Wizards

FUN FACT

Mangetutti-frutti is a vegetable that provides nourishment for Smashlings.

WIGGLES

Wise Wiggles is incredibly caring and nurturing toward all Smashlings and gives the best hugs. Wiggles has a plant-based diet, telling everyone that it eats "rice, not mice." Wiggles' favorite food is mangetutti-frutti.

DID YOU KNOW?

Puggsy sometimes gets a little bit too excited and drools over Wimbly when they're at the movies.

WIMBLY

Wimbly is a totally wild, super Bouncy Baller Smashling that loves hanging out with pals and going to the drive-through movie theater to catch a flick. Wimbly dislikes the rain—the droopy, damp, and extra fluffy look is not the look that Wimbly is going for! Nobody wants to be a soggy Smashling.

About: Speedy, springy, and spirited
Rarity: Common
Likes: Strawberries and cream
Dislikes: Rain
Wimbly's besties:

SHAKEY	PUGGSY	SQUISH

FUN FACT

When Wimbly isn't hanging out with friends, the lightning-fast Smashling tears up the tennis court, bouncing all over the place from one end to the other. It's the most fun a Bouncy Baller Smashling can have.

A Bouncy Baller Smashling

HARMONY

Harmony is a total book bug, so it'll come as no surprise to read that this Smashling's favorite place is the Piñata Village Library. Here, excited Harmony works hard sorting and caring for the many wondrous books it holds. There's also a secret, hidden vault of books that only Harmony has access to—absolute book bliss for a Flutter Bug.

About: Organized, dedicated, and clever
Rarity: Exclusive
Likes: Reading
Dislikes: Late returns

FUN FACT

The secret vault in the library is filled with ancient scripts and books of history and wonder. But Harmony is happiest getting lost in the stories and adventures of regular books.

A Flutter Bug Smashling

HARMONY IS WAITING FOR YOU IN THE GAME!

HOW TO CATCH HARMONY

To add this Flutter Bug Smashling to your collection, visit
www.smashlings.com/codes